1904

SAMANTHA'S CRAFT BOOK

*A Look at
Crafts from the
Past with Projects
You Can Make Today*

PLEASANT COMPANY PUBLICATIONS, INC.

First Edition.
Printed in the United States of America.
94 95 96 97 98 99 WCR 10 9 8 7 6 5 4 3 2

The American Girls Collection® is a registered
trademark of Pleasant Company Incorporated.

PICTURE CREDITS

The following individuals and organizations have generously
given permission to reprint illustrations in this book:
Pages 1, 4 —State Historical Society of Wisconsin; 5—Library of Congress,
Washington, D.C./Courtesy Mrs. Sharp's Traditions Collection of Antique Images
(top); From the Collections of Henry Ford Museum & Greenfield Village (bottom);
7—Used with permission of New Cavendish Books, London, from *The History of
Printed Scraps* by Alistair Allen & Joan Hoverstadt; 9—Cassatt, Mary, *Miss Mary
Ellison*, Chester Dale Collection, National Gallery of Art, Washington; 11—From the
Collections of Henry Ford Museum & Greenfield Village; 12—State Historical Society
of Wisconsin; 13—From the Collection of Naomi and Walter Rosenblum (top); State
Historical Society of Wisconsin (bottom); 19—Reprinted with the permission of
Charles Scribner's Sons, an imprint of Macmillan Publishing, from *Decorative Art of
Victoria's Era* by Frances Lichten. Copyright 1950 Charles Scribner's Sons; copyright
renewed (c) 1977 Ralph C. Busser, Jr.; 20—Library of Congress, Washington, D.C./
Courtesy Mrs. Sharp's Traditions Collection of Antique Images; 21—Library of
Congress (top); From the Collections of Henry Ford Museum & Greenfield Village
(bottom); 22—Jericho Historical Society; 25—George Eastman House; 26, 29—Library
of Congress, Washington, D.C./Courtesy Mrs. Sharp's Traditions Collection of
Antique Images; 27— Library of Congress (top and bottom); 31—The Bettmann
Archive; 32, 34— State Historical Society of Wisconsin; 35— Taken from *Old Time
Gardens* by Alice Morse Earle, published by the Macmillan Company, © 1901;
37—Minnesota Historical Society; 39—Culver Pictures; 41—From the
Collections of Henry Ford Museum & Greenfield Village.

Edited by Jodi Evert
Written by Rebecca Sample Bernstein and Jodi Evert
Designed and Art Directed by Jane S. Varda
Produced by Karen Bennett, Laura Paulini, and Pat Tuchscherer
Cover Illustration by Luann Roberts Smith
Inside Illustrations by Geri Strigenz Bourget
Photography by Mark Salisbury
Historical and Picture Research by Polly Athan,
Rebecca Sample Bernstein, Jodi Evert, and Doreen Smith
Crafts Made by Jean doPico, Kristi Jacobek, and June Pratt
Craft Testing Coordinated by Jean doPico
Prop Research by Leslie Cakora

All the instructions in this book have been tested by both children and adults.
Results from their testing were incorporated into this book. Nonetheless, all
recommendations and suggestions are made without any guarantees on the part of
Pleasant Company Publications Incorporated. Because of differing tools, materials,
conditions, and individual skills, the publisher disclaims liability for any injuries,
losses, or other damages that may result from using the information in this book.

Library of Congress Cataloging-in-Publication Data

Evert, Jodi.
Samantha's craft book : a look at crafts from the past with projects you can make
today / [edited by Jodi Evert ; written by Jodi Evert and Rebecca Sample Bernstein ;
inside illustrations by Geri Strigenz Bourget ; photography by Mark Salisbury]. —
1st ed.
p. cm.
ISBN 1-56247-115-5 (softcover)
1. Handicraft—Juvenile literature. 2. United States—Social life and customs—
20th century—Juvenile literature. [1. Handicraft. 2. United States—Social life
and customs—20th century.]
I. Bernstein, Rebecca Sample. II. Strigenz, Geri K., ill. III. Salisbury, Mark, ill. IV. Title.
TT171.E94 1994 745.5—dc20 94-12058 CIP AC

CONTENTS

S pecial thanks to all the children and adults who tested the crafts and gave us their valuable comments:

Nicole Anderson and her mother Nancy Anderson
Stephanie Auen and her mother Carolyn Schoenwald
Jessica Baumgarten and her mother Rose Baumgarten
Samantha Bechmann and her mother Sheila Bechmann
Samantha Golden and her mother Barbara Golden
Ellen Hauschen and her father Paul Hauschen
Emily Holler and her mother Lana Holler
Katherine Huber and her mother Jennifer Huber
Kari Jordan and her mother Karen Jordan
Michael Kittle and his mother Denise Kittle
Mary Minahan and her mother Lisa Minahan
Emily Morrison and her mother Kim Morrison
Meghan Moyer and her mother Deb Moyer
Clara Neale and her mother Chris Neale
Chelsea Osterby and her mother Barbara Schwarz
Sophia Ott and her mother Peggy Scott
Kati Peiss and her mother Kristi Peiss
Sarah Peterson and her mother Nan Peterson
Megan Petrie and her mother Mary Petrie
Lindsay Polasek and her mother Lori Jolin Polasek
Christina Quale and her mother Monica Quale
Terra Randall and her mother Laura-Jane Randall
Clarlie Rasmussen and her mother Faye Rasmussen
Lauren Roberts and her mother Karen Roberts
Diana Rodriguez and her mother Celina Kobs
Meghan Rohde and her mother Karen Rohde
Mollie Rostad and her mother Genie Campbell
Monica Saidler and her mother Elyse Saidler
Dawn Schwartz and her mother Shelley Schwartz
Jessa Sharkey and her mother Paulette Sharkey
Jennifer Sharpe and her mother Lynda Sharpe
Elizabeth Skogen and her mother Judith Skogen
Carly Sorenson and her mother Sandra Sorenson
Ashley Strassman and her mother Diane Strassman
Rachel Tham and her mother Nancy Tham
Heidi Tiefenthaler and her mother Liz Tiefenthaler
Ashley and Lindsey Trachtenberg and their mother Ann Trachtenberg
Jennifer Tuggle and her mother Terri Tuggle
Sarah Verrill and her parents Kathleen and Steve Verrill
Caitlin Wichlacz and her mother Jacqueline Wichlacz

CRAFTS FROM THE PAST

By 1904, girls like Samantha made crafts because they enjoyed making them, not because they needed to make them. More and more Americans bought clothes, toys, and furniture from stores or catalogues. And most of the items sold in stores and catalogues were made by machines in factories.

In Samantha's time, factories were changing the way people lived. Many families moved from the country into the city to take better-paying factory jobs. In the country, these families had worked together to make some of their own clothes, furniture, and tools. But in the city, many fathers, mothers, and even children worked in factories to make things for other people.

Factories made life easier for wealthy American families. Girls like Samantha didn't have to weave cloth, spin thread, or sew clothes. And they relied on servants to cook their meals and clean their homes. They had free time for "proper" pastimes such as painting, flower arranging, and fancy needlework. Wealthy girls and women took great pride in making beautiful, elegant crafts for their homes.

Learning how and why crafts were made long ago will help you understand what it was like to grow up the way Samantha did. Making the crafts she might have made will bring history alive for you today.

SAMANTHA ❧ 1904

Samantha Parkington was an orphan, raised by her grandmother in the early 1900s. She grew up at a time when America was popping with newfangled notions and fantastic inventions like the telephone and the automobile.

Girls in Samantha's time learning to weave on small looms.

1

CRAFT TIPS

This list of tips gives you some hints about creating the crafts in this book. But this is the most important tip: **work with an adult**. The best thing about these crafts is the fun you will have making them together.

1. Choose a time that suits you and the adult who's working with you, so that you will both enjoy making crafts together.

2. You can find most of the materials listed in this book in your home or at craft or fabric stores. If an item in the materials list is starred (*), look at the bottom of the list to find out where you can get it.

3. If you don't have something you need or can't find it at the store, think of something similar you could use. You might just think of something that works even better!

4. Read the instructions for a craft all the way through before you start it. Look at the pictures. They will help you understand the steps.

5. If there's a step that doesn't make sense to you, try it out with a piece of scrap paper or fabric first. Sometimes acting it out helps.

6. Select a good work area for your craft project. Pick a place that has plenty of light and is out of reach of pets and younger brothers or sisters.

PAINTS AND BRUSHES

*You'll use water-based, or **acrylic**, paints to make some of the crafts in this book. Here are a few hints for using paints and brushes:*

🖌 *Don't dip your brush into the paint bottle. Squeeze a little paint onto newspaper or a paper plate.*

🖌 *Have a bowl of water handy to clean the brush each time you change colors.*

🖌 *Make sure one color is dry before adding another.*

🖌 *Clean your brush with soap and water and let it dry before you put it away.*

7. Wear an apron, tie back your hair, and roll up your sleeves. Cover your work area with newspapers and gather all the materials you will need before you start.

8. It pays to be careful. Be sure to get an adult's help when the instructions tell you to. Have an adult help you use tools properly. Don't use the stove or oven without an adult's permission.

9. Pay attention when using sharp knives or scissors so you don't cut your fingers! Remember—good, sharp knives and scissors are safer and easier to use than dull ones.

10. To prevent spills, put the covers back on containers tightly. If you do spill, clean it up right away.

11. If your craft doesn't turn out exactly like the picture in the book, that's terrific! The pictures are there just to give you ideas. Crafts become more meaningful when you add your own personal touch.

12. Clean up is part of making crafts, too. Leave your work area as clean as you found it. Wash and dry dishes, trays, and tabletops. Sweep the floor. Throw away the garbage.

THREADING A NEEDLE

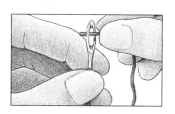

1. Wet the tip of the thread in your mouth. Then push the tip of the thread through the eye of the needle.

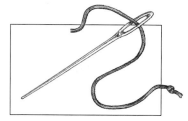

2. Pull about 5 inches of the thread through the needle. Then tie a double knot near the end of the long tail of thread.

IN THE PARLOR

The front hall of a house like Grandmary's.

When visitors came to call at Samantha's home, Mr. Hawkins, the butler, answered the door. He showed the visitors into the front hall, and they waited there while Mr. Hawkins announced them to Grandmary. If Grandmary was accepting callers, Mr. Hawkins showed them into the parlor.

In many homes, the parlor was considered the most important room in the house. It was used for company and for weddings, parties, and other social events. Most people thought it was very important to have a parlor. Even families who had small homes tried to set aside part of a room for a parlor.

Some parlors were so formal that children weren't even allowed to enter them! People filled their parlors with objects they hoped would show how cultured and sophisticated they were. Beautiful paintings and sculptures showed their appreciation of fine art, and collections of seashells showed their interest in natural science. Things they had made themselves, like trinket boxes, paper fans, and bouquets of paper flowers, showed their own artistic talent.

A family in the parlor.

But in the early 1900s, attitudes about parlors were changing. Some people thought it was wasteful to have a room that was used only for company. Many new houses didn't include parlors at all.

Some people who had parlors tried to make them homier and more welcoming. They gathered in the parlor to talk, read, and relax in the evenings. They thought more about how to make their homes comfortable and less about how their homes might impress other people.

IN THE PARLOR

෧

Trinket Box

•

Fancy Fan

•

Glass Paperweight

CALLING CARDS

*Women often went **calling**, or visiting friends, in the afternoon. If a friend was not home, a visitor left a calling card. People kept special dishes called **card receivers** in their front halls. These dishes were made just for holding calling cards.*

TRINKET BOX

Little boxes covered with colorful paper scraps decorated many parlor tables.

MATERIALS

Sandpaper
Unfinished wooden box with lid, 3 by 4 inches
2 foam paintbrushes, each 1 inch wide
Acrylic paint, any color
Scissors
Old magazines or greeting cards
White glue
Small bowl

DIRECTIONS

1. Lightly sand the wooden box and lid. Wipe away the dust. Use 1 of the foam paintbrushes to paint the box and lid inside and out.

2. Set both the box and lid aside to dry. Keep the lid off the box. You'll need to keep them separate until the very end of this project.

3. Cut out small pictures from old magazines and greeting cards. Make sure your pictures are small enough to fit on the box or its lid.

4. When you have cut enough pictures, think about how you'd like to arrange them. For example, you might want to put your favorite picture in the center of the lid.

5. After you have planned your design, start gluing your pictures to the lid and the sides of the box. Make sure the pictures are glued on completely, with no edges curling up.

6. If any of the pictures stick out past the edges of the box or lid, trim them to fit.

7. Squeeze glue into the small bowl until it is about ¼ inch deep. Dip the other foam paintbrush into the glue.

8. Lightly brush a thin layer of glue over the lid and sides of the box. The glue will look milky at first, but it will dry clear. If the glue gets too thick, add a little water to thin it.

9. Let the glue dry for about 15 minutes. Then give the box and lid another coat of glue.

10. When the glue is dry, your box is finished! Fill it with hair ribbons, jewelry, or other small trinkets. 🐚

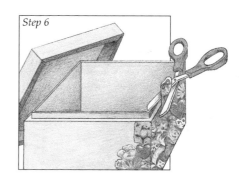

Step 6

SCRAP PICTURES

In Samantha's time, "scraps" didn't mean "leftovers." It meant small pictures printed on sheets of paper. Girls and women cut out the pictures and pasted them into scrapbooks or onto boxes, vases, or furniture. They traded scraps with their friends, too.

FANCY FAN

A paper fan is both pretty and practical.

MATERIALS

Sheet of gift wrap, 30 by 4 inches
2 heavy books
Ruler
Stapler
Foam paintbrush, 1 inch wide
Acrylic paint, any color
2 flat sticks, 8 inches by $\frac{1}{2}$ inch
White glue
Rubber band
6-inch satin ribbon, 1 inch wide

DIRECTIONS

1. Lay the sheet of gift wrap on a table, with the back side facing up. Place 1 heavy book at each end of the gift wrap overnight to flatten it.

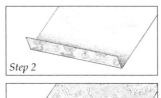

Step 2

Step 3

2. Remove the books, and then fold 1 end of the paper over 1 inch.

3. Turn over the paper and make another fold 1 inch from your first fold.

4. Continue folding until you reach the end of your paper.

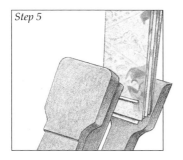

Step 5

5. Staple the fan together, about $\frac{1}{4}$ inch from 1 end.

6. Now make a handle for your fan. Paint each flat stick on 1 side. Let the paint dry, and then paint the other side of each stick. Paint the edges, too.

7. When the paint is dry, glue 1 flat stick to 1 of the outside folds of the fan, $\frac{1}{4}$ inch above the staple.

Step 7

8. Glue the other flat stick to the other outside fold in the same way.

9. Wrap a rubber band around the fan to keep it closed until the glue is dry.

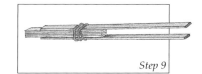

Step 9

10. When the glue is dry, open your fan. Tie the ribbon around the handle to keep the fan open, and untie the ribbon when you want it closed. 🐦

KEEPING COOL

Fans were proper accessories for young ladies during the hot summer months. They were useful, too. There was no air-conditioning in 1904!

GLASS PAPERWEIGHT

Set your glass paperweight on a table or shelf where it will catch the light.

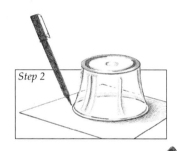

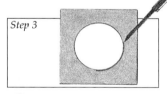

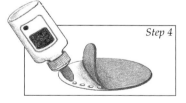

MATERIALS

Small glass bowl, jar, or votive candleholder
Piece of poster board, 5 inches square
Black marker or pen
Scissors
Piece of felt, 5 inches square
Fabric glue
Small objects, such as dried flowers, stones, shells,
    pinecones, or toys
Piece of satin cord, 12 inches long

DIRECTIONS

1. Place the glass container upside down on the poster board.

2. Use the black marker or pen to trace around the container. Cut out the outline.

3. Place the poster board outline on the felt square. Use the black marker or pen to trace around the poster board, and then cut out the felt.

4. Dot glue around the edges of the poster board. Then glue the felt to the poster board. Make sure the edges of the felt and poster board are lined up.

5. Decide what you'd like to put inside your paperweight. You may want to use 1 object, such as a beautiful polished stone or tiny doll. Or you may want to make an arrangement of several objects.

6. When you're happy with your arrangement, place the glass container over the arrangement to make sure everything fits.

7. Remove the glass container. Glue your object or objects to the felt. Let the glue dry for a few minutes.

8. Squeeze small dots of glue around the edges of the felt. Place the glass container upside down onto the glue. Make sure the edges of the glass container line up with the edges of the felt.

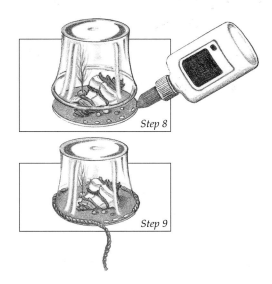

Step 8

9. Glue the satin cord around the bottom edge of your paperweight. Cut off any extra cord.

Step 9

10. When the glue is dry, your paperweight is complete! ❧

COLLECTIONS UNDER GLASS

*In the early 1900s, collecting things like flowers, shells, seeds, and butterflies was a popular pastime. Girls and women displayed their families' collections under glass domes called **shades**.*

A STITCH IN TIME

Sewing in the parlor.

Each day at four o'clock, Samantha went to the parlor for her sewing hour with Grandmary. She practiced fancy embroidery on samplers and handkerchiefs while Grandmary worked on more difficult projects like tablecloths.

In 1904, wealthy women and girls did fancy sewing for entertainment and to make decorations for their homes. They didn't sew practical things like clothes. Most well-to-do women like Grandmary had sewing machines, and they often hired a seamstress to make their families' clothes.

Jessie was the seamstress who made all the clothes for Grandmary's household. Whenever Samantha got into mischief and tore a hole in her stocking, she knew Jessie would help her. Best of all, Jessie would never breathe a word to Grandmary about it! Some seamstresses lived in their employers' home. But most, like Jessie, worked in their employers' home during the day and went home at night.

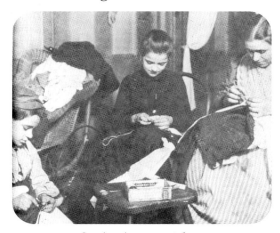

Sewing in a sweatshop.

By the early 1900s, more and more clothing was being made outside the home. Skilled seamstresses were being replaced by men, women, and children making clothes in factories or in *sweatshops*, which were usually warehouses or lofts that were poorly lit and poorly heated.

Unlike Jessie, sweatshop workers didn't make a whole item of clothing. Each worker had a different job to do. Some workers cut pattern pieces and others sewed them together. Then *outworkers*, or women and their daughters who worked from their homes, picked up bundles of unfinished clothes and took them home. They sewed hems until it was too dark to see. A whole family might earn as little as two dollars for one week's work.

A STITCH IN TIME

☙

Heart-Shaped Sachet

•

Embroidered Handkerchief

•

Toss Pillow

SEWING MACHINES

In the early 1900s, sewing machines helped seamstresses make clothes more easily. They also helped factories make clothes more inexpensively and quickly than a seamstress ever could.

HEART-SHAPED SACHET

Make a heart-shaped sachet for Valentine's Day.

MATERIALS

Pencil
Sheet of tracing paper
Scissors
Straight pins
Piece of cotton fabric, 5 inches square
Piece of lace, 5 inches square
Ruler
Thread to match fabric
Needle
Spoon
Potpourri
7-inch piece of ribbon, $1/8$ inch wide

DIRECTIONS

1. Use the pencil to trace the heart pattern shown on page 42 onto tracing paper. Then cut it out.

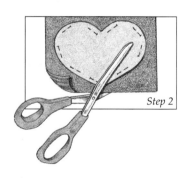
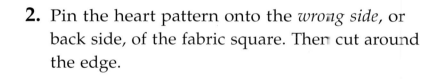

2. Pin the heart pattern onto the *wrong side*, or back side, of the fabric square. Then cut around the edge.

3. Unpin the pattern. Then cut out a heart from the lace in the same way.

4. Lay the fabric heart on the table with the *right side*, or front side, facing up.

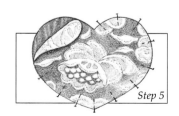
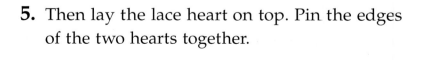

5. Then lay the lace heart on top. Pin the edges of the two hearts together.

6. Cut an 18-inch piece of thread, and then thread the needle. Tie a double knot at 1 end of the thread.

7. Backstitch the hearts together, $\frac{1}{4}$ inch from the edge. To backstitch, come up at A and then go down at B.

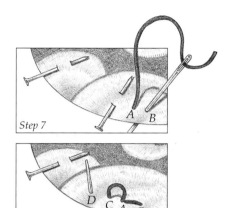

Step 7

8. Come up at C. Then go down at A and come up at D.

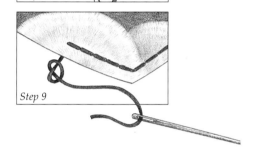

Step 8

9. Keep stitching until there are 2 inches left open. Then tie a knot close to your last stitch and cut off the extra thread.

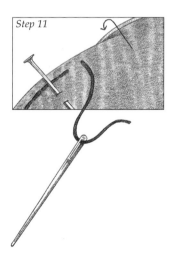

Step 9

10. Unpin the fabric and turn it inside out. Spoon potpourri into the sachet until it's plump.

11. Tuck the raw edges of fabric inside the sachet. Pin the edges together and finish sewing them up.

Step 11

12. Remove the pins. For a finishing touch, tie a small ribbon bow and sew it to the top of the sachet. 🕊

From the book *Changes for Samantha*

VALENTINES

*In 1904, girls made valentines from doilies, ribbons, and colorful paper scraps. They sent valentines to everyone they cared about. There was a new kind of valentine, too. It was called the **penny dreadful** because it cost a penny and had a funny or sassy message.*

EMBROIDERED HANDKERCHIEF

Handkerchiefs were part of a well-dressed young lady's outfit when Samantha was a girl.

MATERIALS

Pencil
Piece of tracing paper, 5 inches square
White cotton handkerchief with lace edges,
  washed and ironed
Piece of fabric tracing paper, 5 inches square
  (Dritz® Mark-B-Gone is 1 brand.)
Ballpoint pen
Embroidery hoop, 4 inches wide
Scissors
Ruler
Embroidery floss *(in dark green and light green)*
Embroidery needle

DIRECTIONS

Steps 2, 3, 4

1. Use the pencil to trace the ivy pattern shown on page 42 onto the middle of the tracing paper.

2. Lay the handkerchief flat on a table. Place the square of fabric tracing paper in 1 corner.

3. Lay the sheet of tracing paper, design side up, on top of the fabric tracing paper.

4. Trace the pattern firmly with a ballpoint pen. Then remove both sheets of tracing paper.

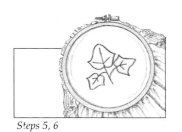

Steps 5, 6

5. Take the embroidery hoop apart by loosening the screw. Place the handkerchief over the inner hoop so that the ivy is inside the hoop.

6. Snap the outer hoop over the fabric and inner hoop, and then tighten the screw.

7. Cut an 18-inch piece of the dark green floss. The floss is made up of 6 strands. When you embroider, you use only 2 strands. Separate 2 strands.

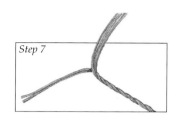

8. Thread the needle with the 2 strands. Tie a double knot at the other end of the floss.

9. Backstitch the stems and veins of the ivy leaves. To backstitch, come up at A and go down at B.

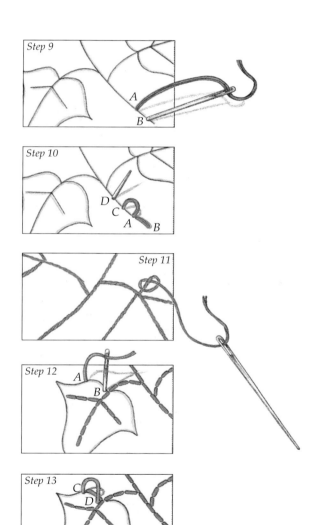

10. Come up at C. Then go down at A and come up at D. Keep stitching!

11. When you finish, tie a knot under the fabric close to your last stitch. Cut off the extra thread.

12. Use the satin stitch to fill in the leaves with light green embroidery floss. To satin stitch, come up at A and go down at B.

13. Then come up at C and go down at D. No fabric should show between your stitches. Keep stitching until all the leaves are filled in.

14. When you finish, tie a knot under the fabric close to your last stitch. Cut off the extra thread.

15. Remove the embroidery hoop, and your handkerchief is finished! 🍃

TOSS PILLOW

Tasseled toss pillows look just as good in your living room as they did in Samantha's parlor.

MATERIALS

2 pieces of fabric, each 12 inches square
Straight pins
Scissors
Ruler
Thread to match fabric
Needle
Polyester stuffing
4 tassels

DIRECTIONS

1. Lay 1 piece of fabric on a table with the *right side*, or front side, facing up.

2. Place the other piece of fabric on top, with the *wrong side*, or back side, facing up.

3. Pin the squares together along 3 sides.

Step 3

4. Cut an 18-inch piece of thread, and then thread the needle. Tie a double knot at 1 end of the thread.

5. Sew running stitches along the 3 pinned sides, ¼ inch from the edge. To make running stitches, come up at A and go down at B.

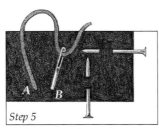
Step 5

6. Come up at C and go down at D. When you finish stitching, tie a knot close to your last stitch and cut off the extra thread.

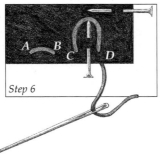
Step 6

7. Unpin the fabric and turn the pillow right side out. Fill the pillow with stuffing until it's plump.

8. Then fold in the last edges of the pillow and pin them together. Sew the pillow closed.

9. Remove the pins. Finish your toss pillow by sewing colorful tassels onto the corners. ❧

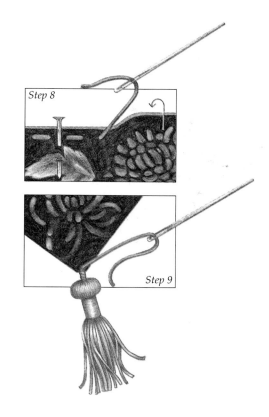

TURKISH CORNERS

In 1904, Americans were fascinated by exotic, faraway countries like Turkey. Some homes had a corner that was decorated in a Turkish style. It was filled with pillows of all sizes and decorated with rich carpets and tapestries.

WINTER PASTIMES

Children playing in snow in the early 1900s.

Samantha rubbed a circle of frost from her bedroom windowpane and peeked outside. The morning sun shone brightly, and Mount Bedford was covered with a blanket of snow. Samantha couldn't imagine a more perfect day for sledding. Grandmary didn't think sledding was very ladylike. But ever since Cornelia had convinced her that it was good, wholesome exercise, Grandmary's stern ideas had been melting away.

After a morning of sledding, Samantha liked to warm up in the kitchen. Mrs. Hawkins usually had a pot of hot cocoa ready and waiting. Mrs. Hawkins sometimes helped Samantha make a "scientific" experiment in the kitchen. They made candy crystals from sugar and water. When Samantha held the crystals up to the light, they sparkled just like the icicles that hung from the roof. The best part of the experiment was eating it!

In the evenings, Samantha and Grandmary spent time together in the parlor. They warmed themselves beside the cheery fire Mr. Hawkins made. Grandmary read by the light of a gas lamp while Samantha cut out lacy paper snowflakes or looked at pictures in her *stereoscope*. When she put in a special picture, called a *stereograph*, the stereoscope made it look three-dimensional.

A woman looking into a stereoscope.

If Samantha and Grandmary had company, they might "have a sing" around the piano or play parlor games like charades and *tableaux vivants* (ta-BLOW vee-VAHN), which means "living pictures." People posed as famous paintings or sculptures, and everyone had to guess which painting or sculpture they were. Samantha also loved to make silhouettes to add to her scrapbook. Uncle Gard was her favorite subject. He always made the funniest faces!

WINTER PASTIMES

Paper Snowflakes

•

Candy Crystals

•

Silhouettes

INDOOR FUN

In the wintertime, some families played indoor versions of outdoor summer games. They played Ping-Pong, an indoor version of lawn tennis, on their dining-room tables. There were even special archery sets made for the parlor!

PAPER SNOWFLAKES

Lacy paper snowflakes twinkle with glitter!

MATERIALS

Small round plate
Sheet of white drawing paper
Pencil
Scissors
Glue
Glitter

DIRECTIONS

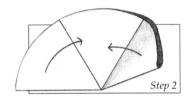
Step 2

1. Lay the plate upside down on the drawing paper. Use the pencil to trace around the plate. Then cut out the circle and fold it in half.

2. Ask an adult to help you draw lines that divide the half circle into 3 equal parts. Fold the paper along these lines. You will end up with a shape that looks like a wedge of pie.

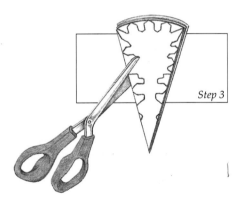
Step 3

3. Fold this wedge in half. Draw shapes on all 3 edges of the wedge, and then cut them out.

4. Unfold the paper to see the beautiful snowflake you've made! Decorate it with glitter. Then make more snowflakes! ๑

THE SNOWFLAKE MAN

*In 1885, Wilson Bently took the first photograph of a snowflake through a microscope. Over the next 50 years, he took more than 4,500 **photo-micrographs**, which are still used to study snowflakes today.*

CANDY CRYSTALS

MATERIALS

1 cup water
3 cups white sugar
Small saucepan
Wooden spoon
3 drinking glasses
Food coloring (optional)
3 cotton cords, each 10 inches long
3 pencils
Small plate

Sparkling candy crystals make a sweet treat for icy winter days.

DIRECTIONS

1. Pour the water and 2 cups of sugar into the saucepan. Heat the sugar water over medium-high heat until it *boils*, or bubbles rapidly.

2. Stir until the sugar dissolves. The water will be clear. Add the remaining sugar a little at a time until it won't dissolve anymore.

3. Turn off the heat. Let the sugar water cool for 15 minutes. Then ask an adult to pour the sugar water into the glasses. Mix in food coloring if you like.

4. Tie 1 end of each cotton cord around each pencil. Then lay the pencils across the tops of the glasses. Let the cords hang down into the sugar water.

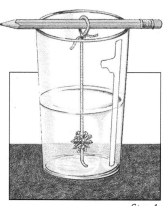

Step 4

5. In a day or so, candy crystals will form on the cords. Lift the cords out of the glasses and let the crystals harden on the plate. Enjoy! 🐦

SILHOUETTES

Make a silhouette of someone you love!

MATERIALS

Chair
Desk lamp
Table
Masking tape
2 sheets of white paper, each 11 by 14 inches
Pencil
Scissors
Sheet of black paper, 11 by 14 inches
White crayon or piece of white chalk
Glue

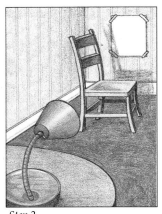

Step 2

Step 4

DIRECTIONS

1. Place the chair sideways about 1 foot from a blank wall.

2. Place the lamp on a table about 5 feet from the chair. Shine the lamp onto the wall.

3. Seat a friend or family member in the chair. You should see your subject's shadow on the wall.

4. Tape a sheet of white paper to the wall so it catches your subject's shadow. You may need to move your subject or the lamp until the shadow fits onto the sheet of paper.

5. When the shadow fits on the paper, use a pencil to trace the outline carefully. Make sure your subject sits absolutely still!

6. After you've finished the outline, untape the paper from the wall.

7. Cut out the outline. Then lay it on top of the sheet of black paper.

8. Use the white crayon or piece of white chalk to trace around your subject's outline.

Step 8

9. Carefully cut out the outline. You've made a silhouette!

10. Glue the silhouette onto the other sheet of white paper. Frame it and hang it on the wall, or start a silhouette scrapbook! 🙰

PHOTOGRAPHY

In 1900, Kodak Company produced the "Brownie," the first camera made especially for children. It cost one dollar. For the first time, many children could take snapshots of family members and friends with their own cameras.

AMUSEMENTS

Children blowing bubbles.

Samantha loved to play with Nellie, a servant girl who came from the city to work next door at the Rylands'. After Nellie finished her chores, she and Samantha met in the secret tunnel in the lilac bushes. They talked to each other on their tin-can telephone, made small baskets of flowers, and practiced blowing soap bubbles. If Eddie Ryland came by to tease them, they blew bubbles at him to make him go away.

When Nellie had lived in the city, she had worked in a factory and didn't have much time to play. In Samantha's time, many adults worked hard to pass laws that said children could no longer work in factories. They thought all children should have time to go to school and to play.

A girls' playground in Samantha's time.

Children like Samantha enjoyed rolling hoops along the sidewalk and playing sports like lawn tennis, archery, and croquet. Croquet was so popular that some croquet sets were made with candleholders in the *wickets*, or metal hoops, so the game could be played after dark.

In big cities, most children didn't have lawns for playing games. Instead, they played on sidewalks or in the streets. In the early 1900s, many people thought it was important for all children to have a safe place to play. They built playgrounds with sandboxes, slides, and swings. Sometimes boys and girls had separate playgrounds.

On Saturday afternoons, some city children and their families went to small theaters called *nickelodeons*. For a nickel, they could watch a 15-minute silent movie. The pictures jumped around so much that children called these movies *flickers*. Just for fun, the owner of a nickelodeon might make the movies go slower or faster, or even might run them backward!

AMUSEMENTS

❧

Walnut-Shell Surprises

•

May Basket

•

Hoop and Stick

•

Soap Bubbles

AMUSEMENT PARKS

*In 1904, a ride on a Ferris wheel or carousel cost ten cents. The idea for the roller coaster, called a **scenic railway** in 1904, came from the trains people rode in the cities. But the roller coaster had more turns and much bigger dips!*

WALNUT-SHELL SURPRISES

Walnut shells make perfect hiding places for tiny treasures.

MATERIALS

Walnut
Small knife
Nutpick *(optional)*
Fabric glue
Gold or silver foil
Scissors
Scrap of felt, ¹/₂ inch square
2 strips of ¹/₄-inch-wide lace, each 4 inches long
12-inch piece of ribbon, ¹/₈ inch wide
Tiny objects, such as toys, candies, or pictures, to fit inside the walnut

DIRECTIONS

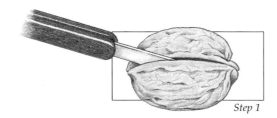

Step 1

1. Ask an adult to help you open the walnut shell. Insert the point of the knife into the crack of the walnut shell, and then gently pry it open.

2. Have an adult help you use the knife or nutpick to clean out the shell.

3. Squeeze a few dots of glue onto the inside of each shell half.

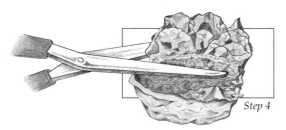

Step 4

4. Line the inside of each shell half with foil. Trim off the extra foil.

5. Put the shell halves back together, just as they were before the shell was opened.

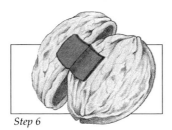

Step 6

6. To make a hinge for the shell, glue the felt square over both halves of the walnut shell.

7. Glue a strip of lace around the outside edge of each shell half. Trim off any extra lace.

8. Glue a piece of ribbon around each strip of lace. Then make a small ribbon bow and glue it to the front of the lower shell half.

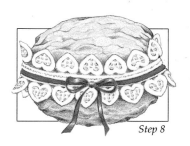

Step 8

9. Fill your walnut shell with tiny toys, candies, or small pictures, and then give it to a friend! 🐿

"Down came the nuts"

NUTTING PARTIES

Families in Samantha's time sometimes had nut-gathering contests. The person who collected the most nuts was called "the little red squirrel." After the contest, most of the nuts were left outside for the real squirrels.

MAY BASKET

*Make a beautiful basket
to celebrate spring!*

MATERIALS

Pencil
Sheet of tracing paper
Newspaper
Piece of white poster board, 12 inches square
Scissors
Glue
6 paper clips
Foam paintbrush, 1 inch wide
Acrylic paints, any colors
Small artist's paintbrush
Any of the following: lace, ribbon, gold or silver foil,
   or small cutout pictures

DIRECTIONS

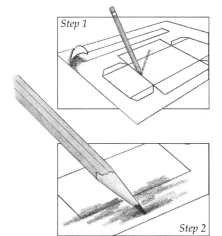

Step 1

Step 2

1. Use the pencil to trace the basket and handle patterns shown on page 43 onto tracing paper. Don't cut out the patterns.

2. Place the sheet of tracing paper onto newspaper, design side down. Use the side of the pencil to color over the back of the pattern.

3. Place the tracing paper on the white poster board, design side up. Then draw over the lines of the patterns, pressing firmly.

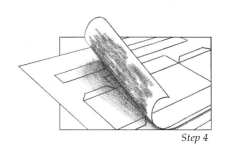

Step 4

4. Lift the tracing paper. The pencil markings from the back of the tracing paper will come off where you traced.

5. Cut out the poster-board patterns. Lay the basket pattern on a table, design side up.

6. Fold up the small flaps, and fold up the short sides of the basket. Then fold up the long sides of the basket.

7. Squeeze 3 small dots of glue onto the outside of each flap. Glue the flaps to the inside of the long sides of the basket.

8. Slip paper clips over the flaps while they dry.

9. Glue 1 end of the handle to 1 of the long sides of the basket as shown. Slip a paper clip over the handle.

10. Bend the handle and glue it to the other long side of the basket. Slip another paper clip over the handle.

11. Let the glue dry for about 15 minutes, and then remove the paper clips.

12. Use the foam paintbrush to give your basket a base coat of paint.

13. When the paint is dry, add other painted decorations with the artist's paintbrush. You can also decorate the basket with lace, ribbon, foil, or small cutout pictures. 🐚

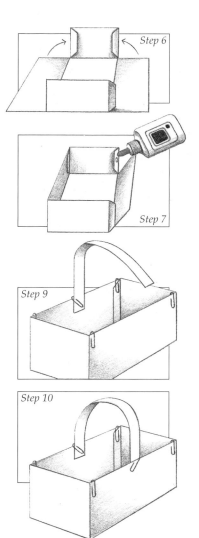

Step 6

Step 7

Step 9

Step 10

MAY DAY

In the early 1900s, children celebrated springtime on May Day, the first day in May. They made lacy May baskets and filled them with flowers or sweets. On May Day morning, they secretly left the baskets on friends' doorsteps.

HOOP AND STICK

Samantha used a stick to keep her hoop rolling straight and steady.

MATERIALS

Foam paintbrush, 1 inch wide
Acrylic paints, any colors
Wooden hoop, 14 inches wide *(The inner ring of an embroidery hoop works well.)*
2-foot wooden dowel, $3/8$ inch wide
Small artist's paintbrush

DIRECTIONS

1. Use the foam paintbrush to paint a base color onto the hoop and dowel.

2. When the base coat is dry, use the artist's paintbrush to add designs to the hoop and stick.

3. When the designs are dry, hold the stick in 1 hand and the hoop in the other.

4. Roll the hoop with your hand to start it. Run along beside the hoop, and keep it rolling by pushing it with the stick. It takes practice! 🐚

EXERCISE

In Samantha's time, people understood that exercise is important. At school, children did exercises at their desks. Many schools started to build gyms and to offer classes in dance, basketball, tennis, and swimming.

SOAP BUBBLES

MATERIALS

1 cup water
³/4 cup liquid dish soap, such as Palmolive®
Small saucepan
10-inch piece of copper wire, 22 gauge
Scissors
Small bowl

*Mix up a big bowl of soap bubbles
and have a bubble party!*

DIRECTIONS

1. Pour the water and dish soap into the saucepan.

2. Ask an adult to help you heat the mixture over medium-high heat until it *boils*, or bubbles rapidly. Then turn off the heat.

3. While the mixture cools, make a bubble wand from the copper wire. Bend 1 end of the wire into a circle about 1¹/2 inches wide.

4. Twist the circle closed, and then cut off the short tail of wire.

5. Bend the other end of the wire into a circle about ¹/2 inch wide in the same way.

6. Ask an adult to help you pour the bubble mixture into the small bowl.

7. Dip either end of the wand into the bubble mixture, and start blowing bubbles! 🐌

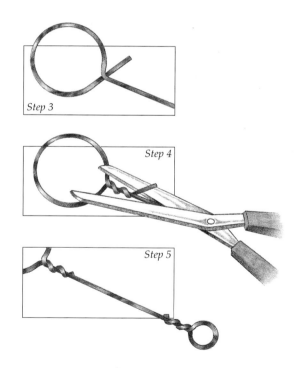

Step 3

Step 4

Step 5

NATURE CRAFTS

Relaxing outdoors in 1901.

I n 1904, Americans spent lots of time studying, sketching, and painting plants and flowers. Gardening was a very popular pastime. People often thought of their gardens as "outdoor parlors." They decorated them with iron furniture, hammocks, and stone sculptures. They thought it was important to have a comfortable spot for relaxing outdoors. In fact, doctors often told their city patients to take up gardening. They thought it helped relieve the stress of living in cities, which were getting bigger and busier all the time.

During the hot summer months, many people left their city homes to vacation at scenic spots like the mountains or the seashore. Samantha and her family spent all summer at Piney Point, Grandmary's summer home in the mountains. Samantha and her friends Agnes and Agatha spent their days fishing, swimming, catching butterflies, and collecting wildflowers and leaves to press. If it rained, they painted or sketched indoors. There was always something to do at Piney Point!

NATURE CRAFTS

Pressed-Flower Bookmark

•

Leaf-Print Wrapping Paper

•

Seashell Picture Frame

Children working in the garden in the early 1900s.

While most people weren't lucky enough to have summer homes in the mountains, railroads made traveling to scenic places quick, easy, and inexpensive. To make vacations even easier, railroad companies built resort hotels along their routes, like Old Faithful Inn at Yellowstone National Park.

If people didn't have the time or money to take a train trip, they could often enjoy nature in city parks. Families could go boating, take a carriage ride, stroll along a tree-lined path, or share a picnic lunch. In Samantha's time, picnics were dress-up occasions. Women wore fancy dresses, and men wore coats and ties!

ARBOR DAY

*Every spring, girls like Samantha planted trees to celebrate Arbor Day. An **arbor** is a place shaded by trees. More than a million trees were planted on the first Arbor Day—April 10, 1872. In some places, people still celebrate Arbor Day.*

35

PRESSED-FLOWER BOOKMARK

Pressed flowers make beautiful bookmarks for your family and friends.

MATERIALS

Small, fresh-picked flowers
2 sheets of white paper
4 or 5 heavy books
Piece of parchment paper, 2 by 6 inches
White glue
Small bowl
Foam paintbrush, 1 inch wide
Piece of poster board, 2 by 6 inches
Small artist's paintbrush
Paper lace cut from doilies
Piece of satin cord, 8 inches long

DIRECTIONS

1. Arrange your flowers on a sheet of white paper.

2. Cover the flowers with another piece of paper, and then slip them between the pages of a heavy book. Stack 3 or 4 more heavy books on top to add weight.

3. Press the flowers for about a week. Check them every few days. If the paper is getting moist, replace it with new paper.

4. When the flowers are dry, plan your design. Arrange the flowers on the parchment paper to make sure they all fit.

5. When you're happy with your arrangement, remove the flowers. Squeeze a little glue into the small bowl.

6. Dip the foam paintbrush into the glue, and then brush a thin layer of glue onto the poster board. If the glue is too thick, thin it with a little water.

Steps 6, 7

7. Place the parchment paper on top, making sure the edges are lined up. Smooth out any air bubbles.

8. Glue the flowers onto the parchment paper. Be careful not to crush the petals.

9. Use the artist's paintbrush to lightly brush a thin coat of glue over the flowers. The glue will look milky at first, but it will dry clear.

10. When the glue is dry, use the foam paintbrush to coat the whole front side of the bookmark with glue.

11. For a finishing touch, trim your bookmark with paper lace and tie on a satin cord. 🐚

TRAINS THROUGH THE WILDERNESS

By 1904, railroad companies were cutting down trees and plowing through meadows to build new railroad tracks all across the country. Women started groups like the Wild Flower Preservation Society of America to help protect America's wilderness.

LEAF-PRINT WRAPPING PAPER

Wrap presents in paper you've printed yourself!

Step 1

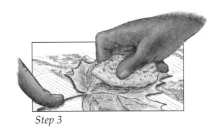

Step 3

Step 6

MATERIALS

Fresh-picked leaves with stems, any sizes
Newspaper
Sheet of white drawing paper
Piece of cardboard, 4 inches square
Acrylic paints, any colors
Small bowls
Small sponges
Sheet of craft paper, 11 by 17 inches

DIRECTIONS

1. Lay the leaves on a sheet of newspaper, with the raised veins facing up. Place the drawing paper and the cardboard square next to the newspaper.

2. To practice making a leaf print, pour a little paint into a small bowl, and then dip a sponge into the paint.

3. Hold 1 of the leaves by its stem. Gently dab paint onto the leaf.

4. Pick up the leaf by its stem and place it on the sheet of white paper, painted side down.

5. Place the cardboard square on top of the leaf and press down. Hold it for a few seconds, and then remove it.

6. Carefully peel away the leaf by its stem. You've made a leaf print!

7. Practice a few more times with different leaves. Try different paint colors. Use a new sponge for each color, and don't mix colors.

8. When you're happy with your practice leaf prints, you're ready to make leaf-print wrapping paper. Spread the craft paper next to the newspaper.

9. Plan your design. For example, you might want to print the largest leaf in the middle of the paper and print smaller leaves around it.

10. Make leaf prints on the craft paper just as you've practiced.

11. When you've finished printing your design, let the paint dry for about an hour. Then your wrapping paper is ready to use. ❧

BOTANY

*The study of plant life, or **botany**, was part of a good education for many American children in Samantha's time. Teachers took their students out into fields to collect samples of plants and flowers to study in the classroom.*

SEASHELL PICTURE FRAME

*Frame your favorite
picture with seashells!*

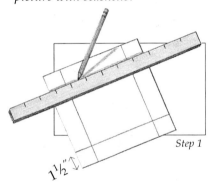

Step 1

$1\frac{1}{2}$"

MATERIALS

Pencil

Ruler

3 pieces of cardboard, each $6\frac{1}{2}$ inches square

Scissors

Foam paintbrush, 1 inch wide

Acrylic paints, any colors

Seashells*

Craft glue

1 picture, 4 inches square

Piece of cardboard, $3\frac{1}{2}$ by 5 inches

Available in craft stores, or collect your own by a lake or ocean.

DIRECTIONS

1. Use the pencil and ruler to draw a line along each edge of 1 of the cardboard squares, $1\frac{1}{2}$ inches from each edge.

2. Ask an adult to help you poke the scissors through the square in the middle of the cardboard. Then cut out the square.

3. Use a pencil and ruler to draw a line along each edge of a second square of cardboard, $1\frac{1}{4}$ inches away from each edge.

4. Ask an adult to help you poke the scissors through the square in the middle of the cardboard. Then cut out this square.

5. Paint each frame piece on 1 side. Let the paint dry, and then paint the other side of each frame piece. Paint the edges, too.

6. Lay the frame piece with the larger opening onto a table.

7. Plan your shell design. For example, you might want to place the prettiest shell at the top of your frame. When you're happy with your design, glue the shells to the frame piece.

8. Lay the other frame piece on the table. Dot glue along all 4 edges. Place the shell frame on top of the glue. Make sure the edges are lined up.

Step 8

9. Lay the third cardboard square on the table. Dot glue along 3 edges. Place the frame on top of the glue. Again, make sure the edges are lined up.

Step 9

10. When the glue has dried, slide your picture into the frame.

11. To make a stand for your frame, fold the cardboard rectangle in half. Then glue it to the back of the frame as shown. 🕊

Step 11

BY THE SEASHORE

In 1904, wealthy people sometimes enjoyed long vacations by the seashore in the summer. They wanted their vacations to be educational, too. By collecting seashells, they could enjoy the beach and learn about nature at the same time.

PATTERNS

EMBROIDERED HANDKERCHIEF

HEART-SHAPED SACHET